The Timetraveller's
Guide to . . .

VICTORIAN
LONDON

First published in 2004 by Watling St Publishing

The Glen

Southrop

Lechlade

Gloucestershire

GL7 3NY

Printed in Italy

ISBN 1-904153-11-9

24681097531

Design: Mackerel Limited
Illustrations: Mark Davis

www.tempus-publishing.com

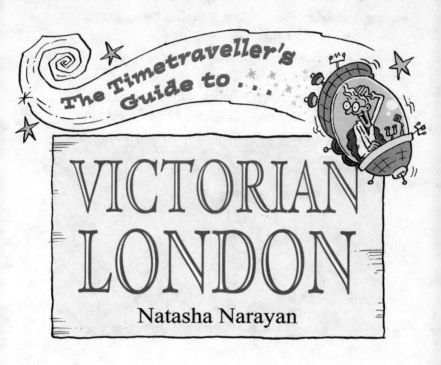

The Timetraveller's Guide to...

VICTORIAN LONDON

Natasha Narayan

WATLING STREET

Natasha Narayan tried her hand at everything from waitressing to apple picking with equal lack of success before she found a small niche in journalism. Her pieces appeared in papers including the *Guardian*, the *Observer* and the *Daily Mail* and she worked as a foreign correspondent in Bosnia, Albania and Georgia. She was also an education correspondent on the *Observer* and, briefly, a presenter on the world's worst satellite breakfast show. She lives in North London with her family.

For my mum, my very own Queen Vic.

Contents

Introduction

Victorian Londoners lived a long time ago – over 100 years ago. This is ages and ages ago. It is *history*. But it is not quite ancient history, like the Tudors or the Vikings. Your mum may actually have had a granddad who was born in Victorian times.

You may live in a Victorian house or go to a Victorian school. If you ride a bike, it's basically the same as a Victorian bike, and if you like taking photos guess who invented the camera – yep, a Victorian.

If you whizzed back in a time machine to Victorian London you might well stroll around the streets for a while – puzzled. Things look familiar. Streets, houses, parks. Maybe even *your* street looks the same. It is still the same noisy, dirty London.

 But wait a minute – it is much, much, *much* dirtier than you remember. What are those great big piles of horse droppings in the street? And that black, smoggy foggy stuff that covers everything in grime and makes it hard – literally – to see the end of your feet. Is it smog?

Victorian London was the biggest, most overcrowded city in the world. It was awesome. Every five minutes of every day of every year someone was born in Victorian London. There were over half a million homes in the city – enough to build around the whole of the British Isles in one long row!

The Science of Horse Poo

The great Victorian urban explorer Henry Mayhew was fascinated by London in all its forms. He was also very interested in dirt. Mayhew calculated the precise amount of 'Food consumed by and Excretions of a Horse in Twenty Four Hours.' Getting his hands really mucky, he enthusiastically weighed the animals food and poo in a 'fresh state ' and calculated how much came out of their rear end to the last ounce. He worked out that each horse dropped over forty pounds of dung a day in London's streets – that is a ton in less than two months. Multiply that by the animals pulling 150,000 carts, broughams, hansom cabs, omnibuses and so on across the city and what do you have? A pile of old poo that's what. Horse poo everywhere was bad for your health – and while ladies and gents could tiptoe through the dung with their noses wrinkled – the ordinary people who lived surrounded by mounds of brown droppings weren't so lucky.

Victorian London wasn't just dirtier than the city today. It was also much rougher and tougher. It was harder to survive in those mean streets than it is today – unless you were fed your baby mush with a silver spoon. That is because there was no help for the really poor – just the workhouse and starvation on the streets. Or you could put your wits to use in a life of crime.

Think YOU could do it? Well read on! 🖝

Chapter One

A Tale of Two Cities

'THE GREATEST NATION ON EARTH...IS IN REALITY...TWO NATIONS, WHO ARE AS IGNORANT OF EACH OTHERS HABITS, THOUGHTS AND FEELINGS, AS ...INHABITANTS OF DIFFERENT PLANETS; WHO ARE FORMED BY DIFFERENT BREEDING, ARE FED BY DIFFERENT FOOD, ARE ORDERED BY DIFFERENT MANNERS AND ARE NOT GOVERNED BY THE SAME LAWS'

WROTE THE FUTURE PRIME MINISTER BENJAMIN DISRAELI IN HIS NOVEL *SYBIL* (PUBLISHED IN 1845).

Who are these two Nations that Disraeli describes?

England and Scotland?
Men and women?
Newly discovered Martians and Earthlings?

Nope, it was the rich and the poor. From birth to death the two nations that Disraeli wrote of could not be further apart. A child of a labourer born in slummy Bethnal Green in the mid-nineteenth century could not expect to live beyond the age of sixteen. (Half the children died before they were five.) On the other hand a child born in Belgravia to rich parents could hope, as one of the young masters of the British Empire, to live to a ripe old age. Do you wonder why? Well read on…

Victorian London was really two separate cities. The West End was the glittering capital of the empire. Smart hansom cabs raced along bright streets lit by the glow of gas lamps. Wits strolled in the park in their top hats flirting with ladies in the finest rubies from India and silks from China. Prim nannies

looked after children in starched sailor suits. And butlers met callers at the mansions of Belgravia, Hyde Park and Berkeley Square. The buildings of empire, Buckingham Palace, the Albert Hall, Crystal Palace proclaimed London's magnificence to the world.

This London was really something. It was the biggest, the grandest city since Rome was capital of the Roman Empire. It made Frenchmen gasp with awe and Germans weep with envy at all the latest gadgets, cameras, bikes and so on, that dotted the place. But this grandeur wasn't the whole story. Only one in twenty-five Londoners really lived in this majestic style.

There was another London. A secret, foul, dirty and sad London. This was the London of the poor. Its heart was in the East End, home to the wretchedest hovels, places like Spitalfields, Stepney and Bethnal Green.

'The East End was...one unending slum,' wrote the American traveller, Jack London in 1902. 'At a market', he continued, 'tottery old men and women were searching in the garbage thrown into the mud for rotten potatoes, beans and vegetables, while little children clustered like flies around a festering mass of fruit... It was a welter of rags, of filth.'

But it wasn't just the East End that was miserably poor. Slums were to be found in the heart of London as the rich moved out westwards, leaving their formerly grand dwellings in Covent Garden and Seven Dials, Holborn and Clerkenwell – when they became too dirty for them too clean. The poor swarmed into these buildings and they became 'rookeries.' Families would live, twelve to a room, in horrible, stinking dwellings with no running water and no toilets. Some families, already crammed into a single room, would still let part of it to a lodger. It got worse. Three people would share a bed. Taking it in turns to sleep in the bed for eight hours – so it never grew cold.

One of the worst rookeries was St Giles, which is just east of present day Charing Cross Road. Charles Dickens, a great Victorian writer, wrote about this slum in his (very long) novel *Bleak House*.

What the Dickens?

Charles Dickens was a great writer, who unlike other great writers, really knew what it was like to be down and out and wondering where your next meal was to come from. When Dickens was twelve, his father, a clerk, was thrown into the Marshalsea Prison because he couldn't pay his debts. The young Dickens was packed off to Warren's Blacking Factory in Hungerford.

This was an awful time for Dickens. He was miserable – doing a wretched job for six shillings a week. He later wondered, 'How could I have been so easily cast away at such an age?' But his time at the factory gave him a real sympathy with the poor and downtrodden. He made friends at the factory. One of his fellow workers was called Fagin and he named one of his most famous characters after him.

Dickens was an enormously energetic man, he later became a reporter, than a journalist and writer. He wrote fifteen novels, ran a magazine and campaigned vigorously against injustice. His novels and stories made him the conscience of Victorian London.

Swells who would walk past a starving little boy with their noses in the air, wept buckets at the death of little Jo, the crossing sweeper, in *Bleak House*. He woke up middle class and rich Victorians to the horrible misery in their midst. There was national sorrow when Dickens died in 1870 and his tombstone in Westminster Abbey read 'he was a sympathiser to the poor, the suffering and the oppressed'.

Dickens' novels are brilliant and his lively characters, such as the Artful Dodger, Scrooge and Fagin have become part of the language. But because he was paid by the word as a young writer, Dickens novels do tend to go on (and on) a bit. Here's a bit of Dickens from *Great Expectations*, a scene where Pip visits Newgate Prison. It is 175 words long…let's see how short we can make it!

'When I looked about me here an exceedingly dirty and partially drunk minister of justice asked me if I would like to step in and hear a trial or so; informing me that he would give me a front place for half a crown, whence I should command a full view of the Lord Chief Justice in his wig and robes – mentioning that awful personage like waxwork, and presently offering him at the reduced price of eighteenpence. As I declined the proposal on the plea of an appointment, he was so good as to take me into a yard and show me where the gallows was kept, and also where publicly whipped, and then he showed me the Debtors Door, out of which culprits came to be hanged; heigtening the interest of that dreadful portal by giving me to understand that 'four on em' would come out at that door the day after to-morrow at eight in the morning to be killed in a row. This was horrible, and gave me a sickening idea of London.'

Haven't the foggiest what Charles is on about in those words? Here is a modern translation. It weighs in at just sixty-four words! You might be able to make it even shorter.

> 'A drunk offered me a front seat at a trial for half a crown. He reduced his offer to eighteen pence. I refused — he still showed me the yard where people were publicly whipped — and the awful gallows. He said four people would come out of the Debtors Door and be hanged at eight in the morning the day after tomorrow. London is sick.'

The filth in London was unbearable. The sanitary reformer Edwin Chadwick found people who had to walk ankle deep through excrement to get from their house to the street. Cesspits overflowed right onto the street. Piles of raw garbage and sewage were a common sight.

Dreadful diseases like typhoid and cholera made a playground of these tenements.

If you were poor you had to take any work you could get.

Seamstresses and costermongers worked long backbreaking hours for very little money. Holidays were for the rich. If you made furniture, for example, you might work from six in the morning till ten at night – stopping for a ten-minute breakfast, a twenty-minute lunch and eight minutes for tea. You would work every Saturday and many Sundays too. A seamstress might make five pence a day and go blind as a result of the long hours at the needle. A slop worker, the lowest type of seamstress, could make just half a penny a day.

The Song of the Shirt

What united stinking rich toffs and dirt poor slopworkers? The toffee nosed and the great unwashed? The answer is clothes. The poor seamstress stitched away from dawn to dusk to make fine clothes for the fancy gents and fashionable ladies. Thomas Hood wrote a famous poem about this called, SONG OF THE SHIRT

Oh men with sisters dear!
Oh men with mothers and wives!
It is not linen that you are wearing out
But human creatures lives

Stitch, stitch, stitch
In poverty, hunger and dirt
Sewing at once with a double thread
A shroud as well as a shirt.

Other writers were even more angry. Charles Kingsley suggested that dread diseases like smallpox were god's punishment on the rich:

'So Lord —'s coat has been covering a group of children blotched with smallpox...The charming Miss C has been swept off by typhus or scarlatina and her parents talk about 'God's heavy judgement and visitation' – had they tracked the girl's new riding habit back to the stifling undrained hovel where it served as a blanket to the fever-stricken slopworker they would have seen WHY God visited them.'

Seamstresses were miserably treated but at least the job was clean. Jobs, like that of the pure finders who scavenged in big dust-yards, like the one near Regent's Canal, for bits to sell – were unbearably foul.

The kings of the scavengers were toshers who went underground into the sewers. There they would wade through filth searching for bits of iron and rope, coins, silver, old boots, anything that had got flushed away. The work was rank and dangerous and there were stories of toshers getting swept away in a tide of murky sewage, struggling vainly to save themselves with the seven-foot-long pole they always carried. There were other, even more yucky stories, of toshers getting eaten by rats and their skeletons being found picked clean of skin.

But being a tosher was relatively well paid – and they were envied by the mudlarks and pure finders. Toshers were a hard, proud and well-respected band of men. It was the working children that lived the most miserable lives. In the 1850s only half of London's children went to school. The other half had to survive doing anything, from going up chimneys, to selling matches, to begging to stealing or to working in factories. Even the pennies that children brought in could

keep their families from starving. Working children were beaten and treated worse than animals. If they fell asleep at work they were dunked in a bucket of freezing water to wake them up.

Children as young as three helped their mums sew on buttons and were kept up until midnight working as hard as they could. Small boys were sent up the narrowest chimneys by their masters, the sweeps. These 'climbing boys' started work at the age of six and often got stuck in the chimney, where they could suffocate to death. The sweeps urged them up the chimney with threats, pins and sometimes even by lighting fires under them.

At first these tots came back 'with their arms and knees streaming with blood and their knees looking as if the caps had been pulled off', a government commission reported in 1863. But their cruel masters knew how to harden them up a bit. They would rub salt water into the bloody skin to toughen it up. This was pure torture. (Have you ever tried rubbing salt into a wound?) One of the saddest jobs was that of the mudlark.

A Mudlark's Misery

I'm Tom. I've always been a mudlark, for as long as I can remember. I'm eight years old. Or nine. My father is gone. Dead. My mother goes out and washes clothes. She's very good to me and does hardly ever beat me. We lives, my brothers and sisters and me together in one room.

My mother comes from Aberdeen. I don't know where that is. We live in London. England is in London somewhere, but I don't know exactly where.

In the morning I go down river with my hat and look for coals or nails in the mud. I fills my hat with stuff. On a good day I'll find some nails or maybe even a copper. People say the boatmen throw out food and ale and such for us to steal — but that ain't true.

I get very muddy and sometimes I cut my feet on the glass and bottles in the mud. I used to have some shoes but that was a long time ago. My feet freeze in the winter. They turn blue. Then I loves to warm my feet in hot water running from the pipe outside the factory.

No, people don't feel sorry for me. No one has ever noticed me. I don't mind. It is good when I finds stuff. Sometimes I even makes more than a ha-penny.

I have two slices of bread and butter for breakfast and a cup of tea. I have bread and butter for tea, the same. Mother eats the same as me but drinks more tea. Sometimes she has three cups.

Henry Mayhew, spoke to hundreds of Londoners for a huge book published in 1861. He met a little orphan girl who hitched a ride into London with a man selling potatoes, after her mum died. She told Mayhew:

'I have been begging about all the time till now. I am very weak – starving to death. I never stole anything. I always kept my hands to myself. A boy wanted me to go with him to pick a gentleman's pocket. We was mates for two days, and then he asked me to go picking pockets; but I wouldn't. I know it's wrong though I can neither read nor write. The boy asked me to do it to get into prison, as that would be better than the streets…I haven't slept in a bed since I've been in London. I generally slept under dry arches… I would do anything to be out of this misery.'

But life in factories could be even worse. Girls who made matchsticks at the Bryant and May factory in Bow, east London, worked in inhuman conditions. Their hands and face would glow greenish bright with the chemicals used to make the matchsticks. Many got an illness called 'phossy jaw'.

Phossy jaw would turn chin and cheeks green – then black. Finally a rank puss would seep out of your face and your jaw would be eaten away. How did the owners at the factory respond when a girl got phossy jaw? They sacked her. But in 1888 the girls finally struck back. After the socialist leader Annie Besant wrote an article describing the girls' sub-human working conditions three girls suspected of talking to her were sacked. All 1500 girls at the factory walked out on strike. It was a very brave move.

Many match girls faced starvation. Bryant and May and unsympathetic newspapers put all sorts of pressures on the girls. But they held fast and the case gained international attention. There was a wave of public sympathy for the match girls and Bryant and May gave into their (very modest) demands. (Such as the right to eat their breakfast in a separate room.) It was a small step for the girls. But a huge one for the rights of Victorian London's poor.

After the strike Annie Besant was asked for help from tin box makers who were being mutilated by their machines and from shop assistants who were illegally fined. Workers began to see that if they got together to protest against slave wages and ill-treatment they could change things. After all, the bosses needed someone to do all the hard work!

CHAPTER TWO

Verminous and Measly Manners

The Victorians were the politest people in history. They had manners for everything from going in to dinner at parties (the host took the oldest and grandest lady in) to going to the toilet. Polite people never, ever mentioned this... um... er... unmentionable... in fact some ladies and gents were so polite you'd think they didn't use the loo at all!

The word hypocrisy – saying one thing and doing another – could have been invented for the Victorians. Let's face it we all use the loo or the powder room as the Victorians called it. These were people who covered up chair and table legs because they thought it was rude to show your legs!

In fact, manners became so important that some people spent hours agonizing over how to lay their table or who should sit next to who at their dinner parties. This was particularly true of rich ladies who weren't allowed to work and therefore didn't have anything better to fill up their time with. So a new profession was invented. The manners coach. This was a bossy lady who would tell you, especially if you were middle or lower class and wanted to pretend to be a real toff, what was GOOD manners. And wot woz not!

Mrs Manners

There were Mrs Manners great and small but Mrs Isabella Beeton was queen of them all. Isabella, who was born in the City of London, was the oldest girl of twenty-one children (it must have been hard work reminding all those little brats of their Ps and Qs). She married young, her husband was a publisher. Which was handy because Isabella went on to write a book called *Beeton's Book of Household Management*.

Guess who published it? Yep, her hubby! This book had 2731 entries, which included loads of recipes that she collected from readers at the magazine her husband published. Plus RULES for everything. If you wanted advice on any of the following Mrs Beeton's your ma'am:

How to give a letter of introduction.

How much to pay your maid.

How to poach an egg.

How to eat your soup.

How to eat peas with your knife (don't ever put your knife in your mouth).

How to eat and talk… 'The mouth should not be kept open in anticipation of the well laden fork's arrival, but should be opened only at the moment when it has reached the lips.'

Never leave a teaspoon standing in a cup!

Here is the advice Mrs Beeton might give JACK, a boy with lamentably poor manners.

'Now Jack sit up straight at the table. And don't speak unless spoken to, remember children should be seen and not heard. No you may not dip your bread into your soup. I know it tastes nice but it shows very, very poor breeding.
Remember what I say in my book "Dip the soup away from you, fill (the spoon) two-thirds full and pour the soup between your lips silently from the side of the spoon, not the tip."No, Jack you may not get up from the table. Dinner is not over yet. A please would certainly be helpful. Very well…but polite people do not speak of the loo. If you really must GO…say you need to answer a call of nature. Have you washed your hands with soap? NO, dinner at Aunt Beeton's is not BORING!!! Well, I like that! If I don't teach you manners who will?!!'

Middle and upper class ladies worried frightfully about their dinner parties – which were a calling for some ladies. The thing to do of course was to have the smartest parties, certainly smarter than that stuck-up Mrs Jones next door. They were glittering affairs, with tables loaded with artificial flowers, white linen and sparkling silver and glasses. The menus had to follow a certain form to be smart. After a clear and thick soup would come the dinner proper. It was considered smart to write the menus in French – though many people can't have had a clue what they were putting in their gob. A fancy dinner might look like this:

FIRST COURSE

Filets de Sole à la Bisque

Turbot à la Richlieu

SECOND COURSE

Les Haunche de Venison aux haricots verts

Les Poulets Diadem

Flancs

SIDE DISHES & ENTREES

Eg ortolans à la vicomtesse

Vol-au-vent de fois gras à la talleyrand

Auiguilletes de petites Poussins à la Banquiere

THIRD COURSE (THE BIG DISH!)

Les dindons poults piques et bardes.

DESSERTS

Ices

Sorbets

Souffles

Bombes surprises

Gateux

Strawberries tossed in brandy

AFTER DESSERT

Finger bowls of water are served with exotic fruit such
as nuts, pineapples and oranges.

Every hostess had a list of people she would invite to her dinners. She would check out that they were respectable and not involved in any scandals – so 'fit to be received in society'. All gentlemen had to be provided with a lady partner. This was difficult if the gent wasn't married because it was considered scandalous behaviour for a young lady to go to a dinner party without an escort. Some bachelors got invited to dinner parties constantly.

The American writer, Henry James, for example, was known to be witty and charming. He dined out in London 107 times in the spring and summer of 1879. He found the constant polite small talk dull – and complained to his pal that he was through with dinners. But when the next round of invites came through he couldn't refuse the hostess.

Irresistible Ices

Agnes Marshall was a cook-inventor. She invented the first ice cream cone in about 1888. And she claimed to have invented the freezer. She set up a cooking school in London and made ice cream *the* Victorian treat.

Street sellers began pushing the first ice cream carts. These were wooden boxes full of ice, on wheels. Ragged kids would flock round these vendors, eager to spend their savings on the trendy new craze – a half penny ice.

Why don't you try making Agnes Marshall's recipe for Victorian ice cream – but be warned it is far richer than a choc ice – too much could make you chuck up Victorian gloop.

ONE PINT OF CREAM
A QUARTER POUND OF SUGAR
EIGHT YOLKS OF EGGS

Put the cream in a pan over the fire and let it come to the boil and then pour it on the sugar and yolks in a basin and mix well. Return it to the pan and keep it stirred over the fire till it thickens and clings well to the spoon, but do not let it boil; then pass it through a (very fine) sieve. Let it cool. Add vanilla or other flavour, and freeze. Mould if desired. When partly frozen half a pint of whipped cream, slightly sweetened, may be added.

While the rich hogged on their poulet de veal whatnots, the poor eked out miserable and hungry lives on very little and very bad food. Poor labourers in the factories or the sweat-shops of the East End had to exist on bread and dripping (i.e., animal fat) and the odd cup of tea.

Elizabeth Killick, an East End sweatshop worker, with three children and a sick husband worked from 6am in the morning till 8pm at night making trousers. Out of this she made just enough to feed herself and her children on herrings and tea – meat was an unheard of luxury never mind ice cream. Hunger drove people to steal loaves of bread, tubs of margarine, or pounds of beef.

For example in January 1888, a young lad called James Cadderley crawled into a baker's shop in Bromley Street, East London on his hands and knees and stole a loaf of bread. Unluckily for him he was caught by a copper as he crawled out of the shop and was given twelve strokes with a birch rod. Even the food the poor had was commonly mixed with everything from sand to sawdust to make it go further – and to make bigger profits for greedy grocers.

Five Victorian Food Scams

- Bakers added powdered chalk to their flour to make it look whiter (it also cost less).

- Grocers added red lead to cheese to make it look like expensive Gloucester cheese.

- Sweetmakers made 'chocolate' by mixing melted wax with brown paint.

- Milk was watered down.

- Food was sometimes foul: Ice cream analysed in 1881 contained cotton, straw, cat hairs, fleas, lice and bed bugs.
(It was a wonder there was any room for sugar and cream!)

No wonder that the children used to sing a little ditty:

Little drops of water added to the milk

Make the milkman's daughter clothe herself in silk

Little grains of sand in the sugar mixed

Make the grocery man soon become well fixed

CHAPTER THREE

Victoria and Her Dolls

Women came second in Victorian London. (If you are wondering who came first it was men!)

It wasn't considered 'nice' for women to work. They weren't allowed to be doctors or lawyers and certainly not prime ministers.

Girls may have been taught flower arranging by a governess at home, but they didn't have to go to school and certainly not university. (The first woman's college, Queen's College in London, wasn't even founded until 1848.) The fact that homes were run and factories staffed by poor women – who had to work – was ignored by Victorians.

Women weren't even allowed to vote for who represented them in parliament. Instead posh women sat at home and crocheted, played dinky tunes on the piano, did needlework, decorated boxes with shells, kept their ankles shapely and supervised the servants (ten per cent of the female population worked as maids and domestics in 1851). They were meant to be fragrant and feminine – like little dolls in their neat little doll's houses. 'Be good sweet maid,' said the Victorian writer Charles Kingsley, 'and let who can be clever'.

The Victorian poet Alfred Tennyson summed up woman's place in the world:

Man for the field, women for the hearth,

Man for the sword and for the needle she;

Man with the head and woman with the heart,

Man to command and woman to obey

But there was one woman who did come first. This was the boss herself – Queen Victoria. She took to being queen like a duck to a swimming pool. She loved the meetings with Lord Melbourne her Prime Minister, she loved the official papers and making important decisions and being very important herself.

Queen Victoria has gone down in history as a stout, beady-eyed matron, spotless respectability. 'We are not amused,' she thunders at any impertinence such as an actual joke. But when Victoria became Queen in 1837 she was just 18 years old. She looked more like a cook than a queen, a funny little hook-nosed, pop-eyed thing with lots of gaiety and passion. Teenage Vicky wanted to be independent – she told Lord Melbourne she didn't want to get married for years yet. And then she saw her cousin Albert. Albert of Saxe-Coburg was a very respectable German prince. Victoria fell for him with a thud.

The Diary of Elsie Botts,
Underhousemaid at Buckingham Palace

Monday

Oooh wot a day I've had. Up at five o'clock to clean the brass wot I didn't have time for yesterday. I knew I'd catch it from Mrs Smith herself if everything wasn't spotless. She's always on at me. 'Elsie have you done the silver?' 'Elsie have you done

the doorknobs?' Elsie, Elsie, Elsie. It's a wonder my head don't explode.

Anyway I's cleaning the candles holders in the Blue Room when I heard noises. I's running late so I nipped in behind the curtains. Who'd you think came in? Yep, it was Her Majesty herself, looking all pink and flushed.

The Queen was with that German prince, Albert. Well you know how I feel about foreigners, but he seems all right to me. He's got a luuverly moustache.

They sits on the sofa and talks in German. I peeps out from behind the curtain and wonders why they both giggle so much and look so red. Then I hears they is not talking so I looks again.

'Albert', Victoria says in a funny sort of squeaky voice, 'it would make me too happy if you would consent to what I wished.'

Albert said he would, in a gruff sort of way. And then they were KISSING!!! That Albert had the Queen's hands in his and was covering them with kisses. I didn't know where to look.

I been on at my fancy man Alf for months, not that he's noticed. You know dropping hints about lovely rings wot you can get cheap. Now I think I'll just go right out and ask him. And if he says it's not proper for a girl to ask her bloke to marry him, I'll say 'well the Queen did it so it MUST be proper!'

Victoria was overjoyed at the engagement. She thought Albert was simply the handsomest man she'd ever seen. When he went to Hyde Park with her, she noted with admiration that he was wearing white cashmere breeches 'with nothing under them.' 'He is beautiful,' she gushed. 'Oh to feel…loved by such an angel…he is perfection; perfection in every way – in beauty, in everything.' Albert, however wasn't so sure. 'Life has its thorns,' he wrote to his stepmother, 'promoting the good of so many will surely be sufficient support to me.' Bertie and Victoria married February 1840. They were very happy together.

And Victoria – although she hated being pregnant – went on to have NINE children. Bertie and Vicky and all their kiddywinks were the ideal Victorian family – the one every Victorian family wanted to copy. They weren't too flashy or too into parties. They loved playing the piano and enjoyed after-dinner parlour games. They were like a very respectable, slightly stuffy Victorian middle class family on a much larger scale. (They lived in lots of palaces rather than a nice terraced house.)

Suffering Suffragettes

In late Victorian times the clamour for women to have equal rights to men grew stronger and stronger. Women nicknamed 'suffragettes' even chained themselves to the railings at Downing Street till the police dragged them to prison. What did Queen Victoria, who'd after all had more than equal rights for years, think of all this. Did she say?

A) *(We must stop) this mad, wicked folly of women's rights... forgetting every sense of womanly feeling.*

B) *I do not wish women to have power over men; but over themselves.*

C) *We women are not made for governing — and if we are good women we must dislike these masculine occupations.*

D) *A woman can hardly ever chose...only meaner things are within her reach.*

Answer: *A and C are Vicky's words. Just because THE QUEEN could choose what she did, it didn't mean she thought other women should be able to. B comes from the writer Mary Wollstonecraft whose work inspired suffragettes like Dame Emmeline Pankhurst. D is from the work of the famous writer Mary Ann Evans. Haven't heard of her? You won't have. She called herself George Eliot to get her books published.*

35

After a time, hard-working Bertie became Vicky's advisor in all things. He grew more and more powerful and *perfect* in Vicky eyes. (Though the English were a bit sick of this foreigner meddling in all their affairs.) Albert was very logical. He loved science and he dreamed up the idea of having a fair where all the wonders of the world were displayed.

It was called The Great Exhibition. Kings and queens, peasants and factory workers lined up to visit the Crystal Palace – a vast glass conservatory in Hyde Park which housed more gadgets and marvels of science than anyone had dreamed of.

After all the happy years together – twenty-one of them – Bertie caught the shivers. The doctors weren't too worried, they thought it was flu. But he got worse instead of better. One royal doc, the brill William Jenner, diagnosed typhoid – a dreaded disease, which starts with a rash. At ten minutes to eleven on 14 December 1861 Bertie died.

The Queen was struck down with grief that lasted for the rest of her life. She wore black mourning clothes – which she never took off and wrote letters on black edged paper. She even photographed Prince Albert's room at the second he died so she could preserve it exactly as it was. Each evening Albert's servants would lay out his dressing gown and fresh clothes and each morning they would bring him his water to shave. The glass from which he had taken his last dose of medicine remained by his bed for over forty years. (Ten years later Vicky's oldest son Bertie caught typhoid as well and nearly died. In fact, it was a plumber rather than a doctor who sorted the problem out when he traced the disease to the newly installed toilet that was contaminating the water. Posh people started to realise the advantages of regular baths and clean water after this.)

Victoria remained in mourning for years and years – causing the country to mutter, angrily, that a queen they spent millions on but never saw was no use to any one!
But Vicky still had an eye for a handsome man.

John Who?

Queen Victoria was much comforted after the death of Albert by the company of John Brown – so much so that wild rumours flew about that she was in love with him. Who was John Brown?

A) A handsome Indian servant. People objected to her affection for him because they were prejudiced against people from India.

B) Her charming secretary who she elevated to an Earldom as Earl Brown De Vere Fortescue Sykes of East Peckham. She insisted that Earl Brown be allowed to build a castle in Windsor's grounds.

C) A fine, manly, but often drunk Scottish groom who took the Queen out riding at Balmoral castle and became her inseparable companion.

Answer: C.

John Brown was a grumpy Scottish groom. He even dared to be bossy with the Queen, telling her if he didn't like her dress 'what's this ye've got on today wummun.' But the queen thought he was brill, enjoyed his bossiness and pretended his drunkenness was 'bashfulness'. She even insisted in 1867 that she would not attend a pageant in Hyde Park unless Brown accompanied her. After Brown died the heartbroken queen turned to another trusted servant, the handsome Indian Abdul Karim who she called Munshi. The court hated Munshi – but Victoria showered all sorts of favours and honours on him.

Victoria lived so long that she outlasted the century. Finally in January 1901 she died after a stroke. Her whole family gathered around her including her grandson the German Kaiser. (A few years later England would go to war with this very grandson.) Henry James, the novelist, wrote how he missed 'the motherly old middle class queen, who held the nation warm under the fold of her big hideous Scotch-plaid shawl'. Vicky had been around so long. No one could quite believe that the portly little queen had really said goodbye forever.

CHAPTER FOUR

Jolly Good Show –
What Ho!

You're rich and your blood is bluer than the river Thames.
You're a young Victorian man about London.

The horrors of the East End, of factories and hunger and
poverty and dirt are nothing to you. You don't have to slave
away in grimy factories or scavenge in foul sewers. Your job is
to be 'civilised' and have a good time.

Life as far as you're concerned is a jolly good show what! As long as your 'man' brings you a decent cup of tea and perhaps a little buttered toast in the morning – about 11am. You might take in the *Pall Mall Gazette* while your valet shaves you and helps you dress. After a hearty breakfast – perhaps kippers, scrambled eggs, ham, porridge, quail, partridge, cold tongue in aspic and more toast – it's time for the business of the day…which is more lounging about at the club.

What Makes the World Go Round?

Breeding and fine dresses might make a 'lady', breeding and well cut suits a 'gentleman' – but underneath all the value placed on bloodstock (and we're not talking race horses here) Victorian high society relied on something much more important. Was it?

A) Cabbage
B) Caviar and Champagne
C) Money
D) Education
E) The Protestant work ethic

Answer: C. MONEY, MONEY, MONEY

Money was what made the Victorian world go round. The dazzling balls, the drawing rooms, the showy carriages in the park, the servants in their splendid red and gold livery – everything was greased by generous helpings of dosh.

The Protestant work ethic (which means that hard work is seen as the best way to spend your life) – didn't bother blue bloods much. Honest toil was reserved for the honest, solid middle class! It was this middle class, and the elbow grease of the working class, that powered the industrial revolution and made England rich!

Pall Mall in central London was the heart of clubland. At the Travellers Club the rules stated you had to have journeyed 500 miles in a straight line from London to qualify for membership.

There were also posh old clubs like the Atheneum and the Carlton which were full of statesmen and lords. And for young bucks who liked to gamble and make merry hell there was the Marlborough Club, founded by Queen Vicks oldest son, Bertie the Prince of Wales. Marlborough house wasn't respectable – because Bertie didn't care how respectable people were – as long as they were fun! The club's members made such a rumpus in the club's bowling alley that the neighbours complained. The bowling alley had to be roofed over and turned into a snooker room before any of the residents of Pall Mall could get a night's sleep. Members of the Marlborough Club included an American swindler and a Count nicknamed 'Sherry and Whiskers'. Count Sherry was a shady character. With the police closing in on him for his dodgy dealings, he committed suicide by drinking poison rather than face arrest and ruin.

His Royal Tum Tumness

The Prince of Wales, Bertie or Albert Edward was a big disappointment to his mum and dad. While Albert (senior) wanted him to study Latin and science and become a man of culture and learning all Albert (junior) wanted to do was to party on. His parents tried and tried. He was kept away from other boys and endlessly taught lessons of huge dullness. But Bertie just wouldn't learn. Mum was not impressed: 'I only hope that [Bertie] will meet with some severe lesson to shame him out of his ignorance and dullness,' the Queen wrote in a letter to Bertie's sister, the Princess Royal. 'His nose and mouth are too enormous... he really is anything but good looking, that [hairstyle] is really too ridiculous with his small head and enormous features.'

Once he escaped mum's critical eye Bertie took to chasing pleasure – with a vengeance. He hunted and shot, played cards and went to the music hall. He loved horseracing and racy women. He had lots of lady friends – like the actress Lily Langtry – and was even involved in a scandalous divorce case. His long-suffering wife Alexandra, turned a blind eye to his frolics – as long as they weren't too public.

Above all Bertie loved stuffing his face. He used to gorge himself sick. A simple breakfast would include haddock, poached eggs, bacon, chicken and woodcock. Little wonder that he was nicknamed Tum Tum and that when he was crowned King his waist measured forty-eight inches – the same as his chest. Tum Tum also enjoyed hunting and shooting. Once he chased a stag right through the crowded streets of London and killed it in Paddington Station. Other practical jokes Bertie enjoyed were replacing the soap in his guests' bedroom with cheese or putting a cockerel in his guests' bed.

Posh ladies had less time for gambling and night-clubs than their men and more time for the Season. The Season was a giddy social whirl of parties; horse races at Ascot, the Boat Race at Henley and 'coming out' balls. The season lasted from May to December. This was where posh young 'debutantes' who spent the winters at their country estates riding and sewing, first made an appearance in London and were shown off to 'society'. Balls were huge glittering affairs. The chandeliers glittered from the ceiling, the young girls and older matrons glittered with pearls, rubies and diamonds. The wine and champagne glasses glittered with crystal. Only the men didn't glitter too much in their evening clothes.

When the young girls danced the night away with gallant gentlemen at balls it was really like being on show in a glittery supermarket. The mothers and chaperones, who were there to keep watch on them, were assessing the bank balance of every gent they danced with – and the girls chances of catching a fat wallet. As marriage was the only job open to them girls really had failed if they became 'wallflowers' and weren't asked to dance.

The highlight of the season was the four 'drawing rooms' that Queen Victoria held at Buckingham Palace. This was where the new debutantes, daughters of the gentry and nobility 'came out' and were presented to the queen for the first time. Entrance to this event was very, very select and only the very pure minded and the very posh (and the very rich) could wangle their way in. No wonder having your daughter presented at court was the highlight of many Victorian mothers entire lives!

LONDON GUSH

By Our Court Correspondent Penny Slavish

June 10 1850

The scent of attar of rose hung on the air as the cream of the aristocracy, the fairest of the fair, assembled in the royal drawing room at Buckingham Palace. Sheer joy shone in the rosy faces of the fair debutantes as they waited to be presented to Her Royal Highness Queen Victoria. And what a picture the beautiful debs made, with their peerless complexions, modest veils and hats with plumed feathers. Truly no other country in the world can boast ladies of such beauty, elegance, distinction, breeding, refinement, grace, wit, virtue... [*That's enough gush. Editor*] As readers of the Illustrated Gush know, only the crème-de-la-crème of our fair civilisation is permitted

into the presence of her majesty. There must be no whiff of scandal, no taint in the purity of the fair maids presented to her. The ladies toilettes (no not their lavatories, their dresses and makeup) exceeded the height of gorgeousness. Satin, silk, rubies... [*I told you...'nuff gush...next time you're sacked! Editor*]

The Duchess of Blah, in blue velvet studded with diamonds and a train lined with satin and trimmed with bouquets of oak leaves, presented her oldest daughter the Right Hon, Georgina, Countess of Blimey. The Hon Georgina, looking truly stunning in the ancient Blah rubies and a pale mustard satin curtseyed to her royal majesty with such true elegance. Then she took a delicate step backwards, her little slippered feet shining. But then. Reader Be Brave. Disaster struck. The young countess fainted. Was it the heat? Could it have been the strong perfumes? Were the countesses' aristocratic nerves – the result of generations of the purest breeding – not up to the strain? The court buzzed with excited whispers as Her Majesty was seen to frown. Only those of no breeding whatsoever would suggest that the countess tripped over her four foot train – which was trimmed with the palest fleur de... [*That's it...even the Illustrated Gush has to know when to stop... you're history Slavish! Yours, Editor.*]

CHAPTER FIVE

The Ugly Underworld

Not all Londoners meekly accepted that they were born to scrape a pitiful crust for well-fed masters. A huge mob of artful dodgers and cracksmen, beggars and magsmen (conmen) made their living by any means they could. These criminals formed an underworld that had its own code of honour and was as tightly organized as their enemies the PC Plods.

Artful Dodgers

Can you match the dodgy activity with the name criminals gave it?

A) Stealing wet clothes from the washing line

B) Stealing from tills

C) Burgling a house through the window of the front room from the road.

D) Burgling a house.

E) A group of boys would put a knife in the window of shop till a crack appeared in the pane. Then they would remove the pane and quickly steal sweets, food or tobacco from the window.

F) A beggar would fake burns from an accident or the Crimean war by covering arms or legs with a thick layer of soap. The soap would then be blistered by adding vinegar – it looked like the beggar was covered in horrific sores.

1. THE SCALDRUM DODGE

2 PARLOUR JUMPING

3 DIPPING THE LOB

4 SNOWBALLING

5 BUSTING

6 STAR-GLAZING

Answers: A4 B3 C2 D5 E6 F1

The Victorian underworld evolved its own patter, which was drawn upon by other sections of the poor. Some trades like the costermongers, sellers of fruit and veg, were as tight as thieves. Costermongers invented 'Cockney Rabbit', this was a secret rhyming slang – their way of talking to each other without PC Plods understanding.

To be a true cockney you were said to have to have been born within hearing distance of Bow Bells – the church bells at St Mary le Bow at Cheapside. But Cockney came to be the language of poor Londoners. It was spoken by Billingsgate fishmongers and Clapton labourers by Hackney housewives and Cheapside cabbies. It was the language of the streets, the docks and the pubs.

Posher Londoners tut-tutted that Cockney grammar was all wrong and that the way Cockney's spoke was torture to the ear-drums. The writer George Bernard Shaw sent up this whole obsession with 'received pronunciation'.

In Shaw's play *Pygmalion*, Professor Henry Higgins decides to try to transform the flower girl Eliza Doolittle into someone who can fool people that she is a duchess. He teaches her to talk proper – though Eliza complains: 'I don't want to talk grammar, I want to talk like a lady.' In the end Eliza fools the lords and ladies at a grand party that she is, indeed, a duchess.

Does a Cock Neigh Too?

The word cockney is supposed to come from the occasion when a Londoner was visiting the country and saw animals in action for the first time. After observing a horse he innocently asked his country pal 'does a cock neigh too?' See if you can do a reverse Professor Higgins and turn this paragraph of posh prattle into cool Cockney.

What Ho, What Ho, What Ho! Old Reginald had assured me that his binge was going to be a awfully fruity affair. Well, I got togged up in my glad rags and tootled over to his humble abode with my hair in a braid. You can imagine my utter astonishment when I found out that his little soirée had been called off. Yep, that's right old thing. Absolutely scratched. It was a jolly bad show. The place was as dead as a dodo. It was hard to believe that old Reginald had popped his clogs.

Turned into proper Cockney it might read like this.

Wotcher, Wotcher, Wotcher. Me mate Reg tole me straight up 'e woz 'aving a lark over at 'is cat and mouse. So I gets me barnet done up an me ones and twos on and moseys over to is gaff. But no doings. 'Is skindy was orf. It was a bleeding shame. Gor blimey, wod yer Adam and Eve it? Reg was brown bread.

Easy isn't it? No? Have a quick butchers (butcher's hook, look, get it?) at these:

Cat and Mouse – house

Barnet or Barnet Fair – hair

Adam and Eve – believe

Brown Bread – dead

Simple, eh?

Nothing struck fear into the heart of the Londoner like the opium dens. These were held to be places of the foulest vice where innocents would be lured by some nasty wastrel, drugged with opium and robbed. Strangely it was legal to walk into a chemist and buy opium – which is one of the strongest and most addictive drugs ever. Housewives used the drug as a painkiller. Many thousands of Victorians were legally hooked on the drug – it was even given to babies to calm sore teeth and upset tummies.

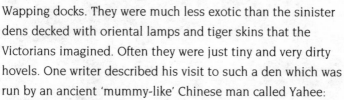

Poets and lords mingled in opium dens with Chinese and Italians, Scandinavians and Spaniards. Some of the most infamous opium dens were in Ratcliffe Highway near the Wapping docks. They were much less exotic than the sinister dens decked with oriental lamps and tiger skins that the Victorians imagined. Often they were just tiny and very dirty hovels. One writer described his visit to such a den which was run by an ancient 'mummy-like' Chinese man called Yahee:

'We see a sorry little apartment… in the centre of which is a common tray and opium lamp. Turn which way you will, you see or touch opium smokers. This cramped little chamber is one large opium chamber and inhaling its atmosphere partially brings you under the drug's influence. Swarthy, sombre faces loom out of dark corners.'

Londoners blamed the Chinese for opium dens. In fact, it was the English who were responsible for the addiction of hundreds of thousands of Chinese to opium. English merchants brought cheap opium into China which they traded for tea. Tea was an even bigger English addiction than opium. When the Chinese government objected the British navy fought and won a war that forced the Chinese to buy our opium!

CHAPTER SIX

Callous Criminals and Loathsome Londoners

Some of the nastiest and most inventive crooks lived in Victorian London. These baddies, as you'll quickly discover, were the lowest of the low, the truly vilest Victorians England had to offer…

1. THE SINISTER SERVANT

Kate Webster was a brawny Irish girl who had started her career as a thief in lowlife lodging houses. Then she became a servant and worked in Wandsworth and Notting Hill – always on the lookout for an opportunity to rob her employers. She particularly preyed on old and lonely people. In 1879, she was sacked by her mistress Julia Thomas – a widow who lived alone in Richmond. Kate Webster hit back – or cut back – by murdering Mrs Thomas with a chopper. Webster cut the body up into bits and then boiled the pieces down to the bone. A foot was found in Twickenham. The torso was washed up in a hatbox in Barnes.

She might have got away with the crime but she was too vile and greedy. Webster tried to sell Mrs Thomas's jewellery and furniture. The neighbours thought it was strange that the widow should have gone away so suddenly – without saying goodbye.

Thomas's house was searched and the knife and bits of charred bone were found. Tiny bits of fat were also found in the pan from the boiling down of the body. Wicked Webster hadn't wasted an inch of her mistress. She had scooped most of the fat into two large bowls – and sold it to nearby houses as dripping. Imagine how people felt learning that they had EATEN their neighbour. (It certainly takes loving thy neighbour to new heights!)

2. JACK THE RIPPER

Jack the Ripper, the person who murdered five street girls in Whitechapel in an 'autumn of terror' in 1888, is the most famous murderer of all time. But if he hadn't signed his first note to the police with the name 'Jack the Ripper' – a nickname the newspapers cottoned on to – he would probably have been forgotten.

The murders were grisly and horrible and mostly took place in the foul, badly lit alleys of Whitechapel. They spread fear over the whole country. Even Queen Vic took an interest. 'All these courts must be lit and our detectives improved. They are not what they should be', she scolded the Prime Minister, Lord Salisbury.

There was a long list of suspects for the killings. They included:

1. Montague Druitt, a barrister

2. A member of the Royal Family – most likely Victoria's grandson The Duke of Clarence, though even Edward, the Prince of Wales, was a suspect.

3. A Polish Jew called Kosminsky

4. A famous painter called Walter Sickert

5. A doctor – because the murders showed some medical training.

The police themselves didn't know who the murderer was. Though the barrister Druitt was top of Scotland Yard's list – he'd had some medical training, was believed to be insane and the murders stopped when he drowned himself in the Thames in 1888. People are still making pots of money writing books claiming they have found the 'real' Jack the Ripper – but we shall probably never know the truth. The problem was the police needed a Sherlock Holmes – and they only had bumbling Doctor Watsons!

3. THE GRASPING GRANNY

Rachel Leverson was a blackguardly blackmailer who ran a shop off New Bond Street called the Temple of Beauty. From her shop she conned the gullible with fake powders and potions such as Magnetic Rock Dew for removing wrinkles and Indian Coal for the eyes. Next to the shop she offered 'Arabian Baths'

and beauty treatments. Leverson liked to be called 'granny'. And her real trade was blackmail. She would lure women into her baths and steal their jewellery – then threaten to tell their husbands that they had been using the baths to meet their lovers.

Many Victorians were so scared of losing their reputations that they would give in to theft and blackmail rather than risk a lawsuit. Mrs Leverson grew rich on blackmail, she had a £400 box at the opera and a grand house near Bond Street.

Granny met her comeuppance through Mary Tucker Borradaile – the silly widow of an army major.

Mrs Borradaile had been persuaded by granny that a rich bachelor, Lord Henry Ranelagh, had seen her at the baths and fallen in love with her. As proof Granny produced love letters she pretended the smitten aristocrat had written. Granny offered to be a go-between.

The marriage, she said, had to be secret because Lord Ranelagh's relations thought Mrs Borradaile wasn't posh enough. Granny and her accomplices pretended that the Lord needed money for some pressing debts – though he was very rich. When granny and her acomplices fleeced Mrs Borradaile of £5000 – all her money – they let her find out that the letters were forgeries. But unlike the other dupes, Mrs Borradaile sued – and gruesome gran finally landed where she deserved – in jail.

4. JEM THE PENMAN

James Townshend Saward seemed the soul of legal honesty with his black silk top hat and flourishing barrister's practice. But unbeknown to his clients respectable J T Saward was really a forger – the notorious Jem the Penman. With his accomplices – who often didn't know his face or name – Jem the Penman swindled thousands of pounds a year for many years.

He worked with a Shoreditch cracksman called Henry Attwell, who would break into safes and steal blank cheques – leaving no trace of his visit. Jem the Penman would then make perfect forgeries on the cheque – he had earlier made sure he got specimens of the signature. Jem then used a network of accomplices to cash the cheques, none of the men doing the donkey work had a clue who Jem, the master forger, really was!

Jem's criminal web spread far and wide – he was involved in the disposing of some of the loot from a railway robbery (see below). He was only finally caught after a blunder of one of his hired men. In March 1857 protesting that he was 'an entirely innocent man' Jem the Pennman was transported to a penal colony for life.

The First Great Train Robbery

The furnace in the back bedroom at Cambridge Villas,
Shepherd's Bush glowed like the fires of hell. It was sparking,
boiling, melting, crackling hot.
It was certainly hotter than
anything these leafy and
proper streets had ever felt
before. Beads of sweat stood
out on Edward Agar's face. He
wiped his face with a dirty rag
and then knelt down on the
floorboards. Carefully, using a
pair of tongs, he removed the
crucible of molten gold from the
furnace.

'Look at it Will,' he said letting the
glowing liquid shimmy gently in the pot. 'Ain't it the most
beautiful thing you've ever seen in your whole life?' 'Aye,' said
William Pierce softly. 'More beautiful than all the ladies in the
Alhambra put together.' As carefully as if the container held the
elixir of life Agar started to pour the gold. But then with a loud
crack the crucible split, letting a stream of sparking liquid fly.
Soon the floorboards were on ablaze. 'Hell,' shouted William
Pierce jumping out of the gold's path with the speed of a
runaway train. 'Help! Help!' Agar had more presence of mind.
He grabbed a cloth and beat out the flames. Just then there was
a knock at the door. 'Master,' came the maidservant's voice, 'is
everything all right?' 'Yes, yes, my good girl,' Agar shouted
impatiently. 'We're having some problems getting the leather
on the aprons right. Go back to your work now my girl.'

It had been a close shave, the floorboards were charred – the house could easily have burnt down. But over the next few days Agar and Pierce smelted down all the gold bars they had stolen from the most cunning and brilliant train robbery ever!

The gang was led by Agar who was a well-spoken, polite gentleman criminal. He had masterminded the theft of about two-and-a-half hundredweight of gold from the South Eastern

Railway company on the 15th May 1855. The railway company boasted that its safe on the train to Folkstone was uncrackable.

With months of detailed planning – which involved duplicate safe keys – master cracksman Agar and his gang of four proved the railways wrong. The greatest robbery of Victorian times wasn't even discovered till the chests – now containing lead – got to Paris! And the gang might have got away scott-free if Agar hadn't been arrested, for a crime that, cruelly, he was innocent of. Languishing in jail Agar found out that greedy Pierce had cheated his mistress Fanny Kaye, who was pregnant with his baby, out of her share of the gold. He was so furious that he turned the gang over to the police.

CHAPTER SEVEN

Clever Dicks and Putrid Punishments

The Metropolitan Police were founded by an act of 1829.
They were the first real police force in the country and were
nicknamed Bobbies. Was this because?

A) They were named after the founder of the act Sir Robert Peel.

B) They wore top hats, coat tails and carried truncheons.

C) They had to walk a regular beat at a steady 'bob' of two and a half miles an hour. Their nickname PC Plod comes from this.

D) Their beat lasted fourteen hours a day without a break, they were expected to get their food from friendly shopkeepers and eat it on their break. Shopkeepers resented their cadging or 'bobbing' free food.

Answer: A. But all the other facts are true, except that they cadged food. Bobbies or 'Peelers' were expected to carry their own food. Plods were allowed to help members of the public but were forbidden to gossip. The very sight of them was meant to make people feel safer.

Victorians joked about PC Plods though poorer Londoners like the costermongers and the mudlarks hated them and accused them of taking bribes from criminals.

The Genius of 221B Baker Street

Sherlock Holmes is London's greatest detective. His deerstalker cap, magnifying glass, apartments in Baker Street, brilliant mind and hapless friend Watson are legendary. Even his arch-enemy Colonel Moriarty has gone down in history. Indeed he is so famous that it is easy to forget that Holmes is made up – the creation of the equally brilliant writer and scientist Sir Arthur Conan Doyle.

In Holmes, Doyle created a character that illustrated the rapid advances in Victorian times in detective work – fingerprinting, the examination of blood groups and the tracing of mysterious poison were all developed during the late part of the nineteenth century. But Holmes was far, far cleverer than any of the PC Plods in the real force.

He boasted to Watson, with whom he shared rooms at 221B Baker Street, that he deduced as soon as he met him that he was wounded in Afghanistan. This he knew by using the 'science of deductive reasoning'. Later he tells Watson that his brother was left money but squandered it, lived in poverty and died after taking to drink. All this Holmes can tell by looking at the scratches and pawnbroker's marks on Watson's brother's gold watch. A 'really logical man' Holmes claims could deduce the existence of the Atlantic ocean without ever having heard of it – because all of life is a great chain. Here are some of Holmes's best sayings.

MURDER LIKE MATRIMONY (MARRIAGE) GENERALLY HAS A MOTIVE.

THE BEST PLACE TO HIDE ANYTHING IS WHERE EVERYONE CAN SEE IT.

A DOG ALWAYS REFLECTS FAMILY LIFE. WHOEVER SAW A FRISKY DOG IN A GLOOMY FAMILY?

EDUCATION NEVER ENDS. IT IS A SERIES OF LESSONS WITH THE GREATEST ONE FOR THE END.

TO A GREAT MIND NOTHING IS LITTLE.

Conan Doyle proved that he was as brill a detective as his creation when he became involved in a notorious real life criminal case – that of a young half-Indian solicitor called George Edalji. Here is how he might have written up the case himself:

Doyle the Detective

Doyle grinned at me as we left the poor wretch huddled in his miserable cell. I have always found prisons unwholesome in the extreme and I confess I felt sick to my stomach as the turnkey clanged the heavy metal door behind us.

I confess, I was flummoxed as to the source of his glee. What we had heard just increased my feeling that poor Edalji's case was hopeless. For once Doyle had backed the wrong horse.

Doyle kept his peace till we were outside in the relatively fresh air. The yellowish smog was choking, hanging thick in the autumn air but Doyle managed to hail a free hansom and once we were comfortably sitting inside he lit up his pipe.

'Well Watson what do you deduce?' he asked.

'The poor man's case seems to me to be utterly beyond hope. He appears so weak that I can only pray that his body can stand prison life. I would not give much for his chances of survival.'

'Your pessimism, my good doctor, is entirely misplaced. Did you observe the letter?' Doyle asked.

'Yes it was in Edalji's hand. The expert T. H. Gurrin identified it.'

'Experts my dear Watson are often fools. The boy did not write it. His capital letters are entirely different. It is a clever forgery.' Doyle paused and leaned back letting the smoke wreathe round the leather interior of the cab.

'Now my good Watson be so good as to recap the facts of the case,' he said.

I cleared my throat and obliged. 'George Edalji, a solicitor,' I said, 'is the son of an Indian vicar. In 1903 there were a series of horrible attacks on horses, sheep and cattle in the area of Warwickshire where he lived. The police, who had suspected Edalji was behind an earlier poison pen letter, had also received anonymous letters accusing the young man of the crimes. They searched his parent's vicarage and found some muddy boots and a jacket with two tiny bloodstains on them. They also found some dirty razors.

A leading handwriting expert matched the anonymous letters with Edalji's writing. Though the bloodstains on the jacket were tiny and the razors were found to be rusty, Edalji was tried and sent to prison for seven years.'

I finished my recital and looked at Holmes, waiting if truth be told, for praise.

'Excellent Watson. You memory certainly does you justice,' he said. Whereupon, to my dismay, he closed his eyes and wouldn't say another word till we reached Baker Street.

Later that evening as I was reading the paper in front of the fire in the flat at Baker Street, Conan Doyle came out of his laboratory. A triumphant smile glittered in his cold eyes and he brandished poor Edalji's jacket as if it was a flag.

'Really Watson this case is no match for my brilliance,' he crowed.

Modesty, I should warn you, was not Doyle's style.

'The mud on this jacket came from a different field. Of course I knew from the moment I saw Edalji that he could not have committed the dastardly attacks,' Doyle continued.

I must have looked blank because Doyle laughed.

'My dear Watson it was blindingly obvious to me, and should have been to that fool of a policeman, that Edalji was so shortsighted that he could not recognize his friends from a distance of six yards. Yet he was said on a moonless night to have crossed a couple of miles of rough ground and climbed many fences and obstacles to get to the animals and attack them in this horrifying way.'

I need scarcely add that Doyle was right and that the young man Edalji was cleared without a blemish on his name. The letters were eventually shown to be the work of an unbalanced young man called Sharp who was packed off abroad by his family.

Though but a small and curious case I do think it provides a good example of the brilliant Doyle at work.

Victorian coppers might not have been as clever as Holmes but they still managed to capture lots of criminals. Punishment for those who were caught was very tough. You could still be sentenced to death for stealing – for example in 1833 a boy of nine was sentenced to death for stealing a pot of paint worth nine pence. Thankfully, he was not executed.

You could also get transported to Australia to work at breaking rocks or digging ditches under the blazing sun or you could be set to hard labour in a convict ship. Most criminals, however, were sent to prison.

Before Victorian times prisons were more like nurseries of crime than places of correction. Government inspectors were horrified in 1836 to find prisoners at Newgate who were so drunk that they could scarcely stand up. In fact, in early Victorian

times, if you had cash, prison could be positively luxurious. You could get meals from the best restaurants and wine from France. You could have women brought into prison to party with you. The King's Bench prison even had thirty different gin shops *inside* its walls.

Victorians were horrified by the inspectors report of 1836 and grim new prisons such as Wormwood Scrubs in West London and Pentonville in King's Cross, were built. These prisons with their awful food and harsh regimes of punishment had a very different feel from the old prisons, they were meant to make prisoners repent and reform as well as to punish them. Isolation was at the heart of this. Prisoners were kept alone in their cells and were forbidden to talk to each other when allowed out for exercising.

At Pentonville the prisoners wore leather 'scotch caps', which covered their whole faces with holes for the eyes. They had no names, just numbers sewn on their uniforms. Prisoners were also given hard but pointless work to make them reflect on the errors of their ways. One particularly horrible machine was called the crank. This was a machine with a handle and a glass dial on the front showing how many times the handle had been turned. The prisoners had to turn the handle 10,000 times in eight hours, or once every three seconds. Every now and then a prison officer would come and tighten the screws on the crank to make it harder…which is why they came to be nicknamed screws.

Victorian prisons were awful. But it is a sad fact that some people, particularly homeless children, committed small crimes just to get sent to prison. However bad prison life was – at least you were guaranteed food and a bed for the night. Innocent people as well as criminals ended up in Victorian jails, most notably those who couldn't pay their debts, like Charles Dickens's father. The most famous debtors' prison was the truly horrible Marshalsea in London.

The Great Escape.
Pentonville Prison, 1836

The prison walls rose fifty feet up into the air, their granite surface slick as a block of arctic ice. At the top they were decorated with razor-sharp, revolving iron spikes. Only a madman would attempt to break out of Pentonville. The guards were so confident they even let prisoners walk in the yard by themselves. So nobody noticed the little burglar, who waited till the guards were changing shift, then slipped barefoot out of his cell into the exercise yard.

Henry Williams was to be hanged in a few days' time. The prospect of death sharpened his wits. He backed into a corner of the yard, then using his feet as claws clambered up the walls. He was more monkey than human as he scaled all fifty feet. At the top Williams hung onto the bloody spikes and worked his way round three sides of the yards. His hands were cut to shreds but he clung on. At last he got to the end and leapt nine feet, from the prison to the roof of the next door building. Then he clambered over buildings until he came to a roof where a woman was hanging out her washing. Williams was a scary sight with blood all over his clothes. But when he told his story the woman fed him and gave him some clothes. After stopping for a pint of beer in Southwark, Williams made his way to Hampshire with sixteen pence in his pocket.

His great escape made Williams famous. But if they had had known his secret the prison guards may have been more careful with him. He had learnt to climb like a monkey while still a lad. Williams had been a sweep's boy whose job it was to shimmy up the darkest and foulest chimneys.

CHAPTER EIGHT

Foul Fun

The Football Association was founded in the Freemasons Tavern in London in October 1863. Eleven clubs met to draw up a set of rules. These rules are still largely played all over the world today.

But the Victorian FA had some wacky ideas. These would definitely be red-carded by any self-respecting ref today:

1. Handling of the ball was allowed.

2. The goal had a post but no crossbar.

3. There was no rule about the number of players on a team or how long a game could last.

4. No forward passing was allowed.

The nice men from Rugby School resigned from the FA because they disapproved of rule 10 which stated there should be no 'hacking' (i.e., kicking) tripping or pushing of opponents. They developed their own game which came to be called Rugby or 'Rugger'.

The first game of FA football was played in Battersea Park on 9 January 1864. Here is how it might have been reported.

THE PENNY DREADFUL

11 JANUARY 1864

Historic game played in Battersea Park

Posh Pariahs – V – Costermongers United

Late stop press

By Our premiership correspondent Gary Spinniker

As footie fans everywhere know history was made today — and yesterday — as the first game of football with rules was played in Battersea Park.

It certainly has been a fantastic demonstration of team work and ball control as the eighteen young pretenders from Costermongers United took on twenty old favourites from Posh Pariahs.

Some commentators have claimed that the tone of the game has been lowered by the Costermongers clan. But there was a frankly superb display of handling by their young captain David Peckham.

'Pecs' superb goals made him the hero of the hour. One particularly breathtaking late number saw him score by throwing the ball at least forty yards. Posh captain Hugo D'Arcy Marcy claimed that the ball was 'too high' to count as a goal...but this was dismissed by referee Nick Neutral as 'sour grapes'.

After fourteen exhausting hours of play everyone was ready to call it a day. Final score United 15 Pariahs 13.

A truly great phase in the nation's sporting history has begun!

When not playing football or rugger Londoners loved nothing better than a trip to the music hall. Music halls were bigger than cinemas are today (no one had the box to goggle at home). The pantomimes and singing acts at music halls like the Empire in Hackney and the Alhambra in Leicester Square were noisy, silly, sad and sometimes fantastical. Artistes like Marie Lloyd and Dan Leno delighted hundreds of thousands.

Audiences of costermongers – who loved the cockney wit of music hall – mixed with slumming lords and ladies. Dan Leno – THE FUNNIEST MAN ON EARTH his posters said – had been on the stage since he was three. He went at his parts like a man possessed by a hive of mad bees and made people weep while they laughed. His songs were zany and surreal:

'Ever seen his eyes,' said Marie Lloyd of Dan. 'The saddest eyes in the whole world. That's why we all laughed at Danny. Because if we hadn't laughed we would have cried.'

Dan Leno went mad playing mother goose – by the age of forty-three he was a sick man. Like his friend the hugely popular Marie Lloyd – who had three husbands and ended up an alcoholic – he had led a tragic life.

CHAPTER NINE

Sickening Schools

Spot the School

Can you match these Victorian schools with the sort of Victorian pupils that went there?

A) PUBLIC SCHOOLS

Schools like St Paul's, Westminster, Harrow and Eton. Public schools had a strict set of traditions and were big on Latin and classics, team sports, uniforms, Christianity and often bullying. 'These schools have been the chief nurseries of our statesmen...their public spirit...their vigour and manliness of character...their love of healthy sport and exercise...they have had the largest share in moulding the character of an English gentlemen,' said a Government commission 1864.

B) GRAMMAR SCHOOLS

These schools were modelled on the public schools but sometimes more practical subjects like science and maths were taught.

C) DAME SCHOOLS

No-one is 'too old, too poor, too ignorant, too feeble, too sickly, too unqualified in any or every way' to run this type of school it was said in the House of Lords in 1860.

D) RAGGED SCHOOLS

'They who are too ragged, wretched, filthy and forlorn to enter any other place...are invited to come here...in the midst of taint, dirt and pestilence,' wrote Charles Dickens.

1. Street children and the very poor.

2. The sons of the 'upper ten thousand' (i.e., aristocrats and gentry).

3. The honest middle class.

4. The working poor.

Answers: A2 B3 C4 D1

The kind of school you went to in Victorian London depended on how rich and how posh you were.

Actually many famous Victorians hardly went to school at all. Many were too poor to afford the cost of lessons – because the government didn't provide free schools like they do today. Others had to work almost as soon as they could talk to help their parents to buy food.

Some kids were taught by tutors or by their parents – or like Charles Dickens, largely taught themselves. The hardly-schooled included the writer George Elliot and the scientist Charles Darwin – the man who discovered how we are descended from apes. Ragged schools, public schools , dame schools and grammar schools all had one thing in common. Can you guess what that is?

99.9 % of 21st century kids would run screaming from them after a few days!

Ragged schools were often held in the most foul and run down buildings. Charles Dickens visited one in Lambeth south London and wrote 'they who are too wretched filthy and forlorn to enter any other place…are invited to come here.' And dame schools were often hardly better. In many cases one old dame would mind fifty or sixty children and her most used bits of teaching equipment would be the cane and the dunce's cap. School days started early, went on and on and ended late. Here is the timetable for the workhouse children's school in St Marylebone in the 1840s.

6–7a.m.	Rise, make beds, prayers, clean shoes and wash.
7–7.45a.m.	Exercises
7.45–9a.m.	Prayers and breakfast.
9–10a.m.	History
10–11a.m.	Arithmetic, times tables
11–12a.m.	Grammar, parsing and diction
12a.m.–2p.m.	Dinner and play
2–3p.m.	Writing in copy books and arithmetic
3–4p.m.	Reading
4–5p.m.	Geography
5p.m.	Supper
8p.m.	Prayers and bedtime

The public schools were for the toffs and the richest Londoners but even here life was no picnic. At boarding school pupils had to endure freezing cold showers, terrible food and hours and hours of the most boring lessons where they chanted Latin verses.

Many Victorian pupils recalled that the most horrendous bullying was rife in public schools. Bullying came to be a public school tradition – encouraged by the system in which younger boys served sixth form prefects as 'fags'. Teachers often turned a blind eye to the horrible bullying believing it would 'toughen up' their pupils and turn them into tomorrow's masters of empire.

The Harrowing Diary of Timothy Brown (aged eleven and a half)

It is half past one in the morning. All around me in the dorm I can see the dark shapes of sleeping boys. But there is no rest for me – I can't sleep for dread of what Flashman has in store for me tomorrow.

Sometimes I think of writing to Kitty or to mater to take me away from this horrible hole. But how can I? Father has saved every penny to send me here, to one of finest public schools in London. I couldn't bear the shame of letting him down. Of destroying all his dreams that I should be the first Brown to be a real gentleman.

This morning Flashman told me that I had better shape up if I wanted to be his fag. I hate him. He may be a prefect but he is a vile, nasty bully. I had to tidy up his room, make his tea and run to the village to buy him some beer. If the master sees me sneaking beer in I will be flogged, but if I refuse to go Flashman will flog me anyway.

I did it. Before cricket practice I had cleaned Flashman's room and got him his beer. I was making his tea and his toast was buttered when he came in with Mathieson and Gilmour.

He made a big show of wandering around the room looking for dirt, under the chairs and round the fire. Finally he turned to me with a sneer.

'What's this,' Flashman he asked. He was holding up his riding boots and they were caked in dirt. 'Is this mud boy?'

I nodded mutely.

'Didn't I tell you to clean my things... Nancy BOY?'

'But Flashman you only said your room...'

'Shut up,' he interrupted 'Cummere.'

I walked over to where Flashman was holding the filthy boots up.

'Lick em clean Nance,' Flashman said in his silkiest voice while his thuggish friends sniggered. 'It's the only way a lickspittle is going to learn respect for his elders and betters.'

I licked and licked the boots and tried and tried not to gag. My tongue was coated with filth, mud and worse. I thought I'd never want to eat again. Finally they were clean — not a speck on them.

But it wasn't enough.

Flashman gave me six of the best just, as he said 'for the hell of it.'

And they say that these are the best years of your life.

Think of the most boring teacher you have ever had. Then try and remember his or her most boring lesson. (I know this is really difficult – when things are that boring you just can't remember them.)

Well the chances are that your Mr Blob or Miss Blank's lesson was much, much, MUCH more interesting than your average Victorian teacher's lesson. Rote learning – i.e., memorising – was the order of the day. At a typical lesson the children had to memorise the principal characteristics of Pondicherry, Amritsar, Madras and Benares and learn the principal towns of France in alphabetical order. Then for a bit of fun they had to calculate the interest on £444 7s 4d at five per cent for fifteen seconds.

IF IT'S FUN YOU CAN'T BE LEARNING!

Religion was big in Victorian classrooms. God was often called in to help pupils learn their lessons. For example children had to learn this rhyme to help them with the alphabet.

A *stands for Angel who praises the lord*

B *stands for Bible, that teaches god's word*

C *stands for Church, to which righteous men go*

D *stands for Devil the cause of all woe.*

This rhyme went on and on… But Victorian children often made up their own ruder versions… like this one which we've made up… (why don't you have a go).

A *stands for Ass, who brays to the lord*

B *stands for Beast, who is ignorant of god's word*

C *stands for Circus, where clownish men go*

D *stands for Doctors, who cause nothing but woe…*

CHAPTER TEN

Inventors and Other Animals

Before the Victorian age people drove around in carts pulled by horses who dropped great big mounds of poo everywhere. After it they travelled in style – in gleaming motor cars. Before it they sat for hours to have their portrait painted – after it someone came along and flash, hey presto – a photo.

The Victorian times were like one of those old silent films. History sped up so events whizzed by very, very fast. Great new cities arose, and great masses of people stopped being peasants and started being working class and fancy inventions like aspirin and the wireless and the bike were invented. By the end London was nearly the London we know and love today.

Here are just some of the people who made London buzz non-stop. (Okay… Mr Crapper may not be one of the most important Victorians – but he had the best name!)

1. Dr Marx, I presume.

Karl Marx, a German Jew, was not born a Londoner. But he lived in the city for years, in a cramped flat in Soho and then later in a new-built family house in Kentish Town. Marx used to stroll on Sundays on Hampstead Heath with his young family and every weekday he made the journey to the British Museum. There he would beaver away in the Reading Room producing his weighty masterpiece *Das Kapital*. This doorstop, which more people talk about than actually read, rates with the Bible as one of the most influential books ever.

Along with his pal Friedrich Engels, Marx created communism, the idea that working people don't have to wait for the hereafter for heaven. Instead they, not the greedy bosses, should enjoy the fruit of their work right here on earth. Marx made words like 'exploitation' – when one person unfairly takes advantage of another – fashionable. His work inspired the communist revolutions of China and Russia and changed the course of the 20th century.

2. Baz's Bog

London by Victorian times was one of the foulest places on earth. Families in poor areas had to wade through piles of raw, liquid sewage to get to the street and even in posh Regent's Street and Piccadilly the old systems of street cleaning was at cracking point. But no one took too much notice till Parliament got involved.

By the long hot summer of 1858 the stench from the Thames, awash with more poo and garbage than fish, was so noxious that MPs inside the grand new Houses of Parliament could hardly breathe and a angry debate started in the papers. 'The Great Stink' it was called. The result was a national competition to clean up the sewers and an engineer called Joseph Bazalgette was given £3 million to build a new sewer system. These sewers changed London. Now hundreds of thousands of people could have water closets (or WCs) installed in their houses. They replaced the horrid old cesspits that used to overflow into the drains and streets. Now, magically, with a pull of the flush...whoosh all their dirt would vanish into the sewers.

Who invented the WC? Was it

A) Thomas Harrington

B) Thomas Crapper

C) Tom Paine

D) Florence Nightingale

Answer: A. Thomas Harrington

89

Thomas Harrington was credited with installing the first WC in the palace of the famously clean Queen Elizabeth back in the sixteenth century. But Thomas Crapper, a London plumber who set up a business in Chelsea, took a lot of the credit. He did not as people still think, invent the WC. It was a stroke of luck for his business (though maybe not for his kids at school) that the first four letters of his name were Victorian slang for the stuff that filled his toilet.

3. Mr Computer

We now take palmtops the size of a wallet for granted but not so long ago computers were vast and people thought they would never catch on. Charles Babbage was a man before his time – a Londoner who first came up with the idea of a machine to calculate maths tables.

The government gave him the astronomical sum of £17,000 to make his huge collection of cogs and wheels and spindles into a maths machine. Babbage got an assistant in Southwark to build the machine – but he ran out of money – and understandably the government would not give him any more.

Matters weren't helped by the fact that Babbage now wanted to develop an even grander 'analytical' machine that could be programmed – in effect a computer! Not surprisingly the government of the day scoffed at such a wild idea. As time went by Babbage became really cranky. He said he spent a quarter of his life listening to terrible music in the street and managed to get laws passed banning street musicians. This silly campaign made him very unpopular. People used to pay musicians to come and perform outside his house.

Still if it wasn't for Victorians like batty Mr Babbage our world would be very different. Perhaps people would pooh-pooh the idea of computers that can talk to each other across thousands of miles in the blink of an eye as mad science fiction! As you've seen Victorian London may have had rotten roads, terrible schools, vile villains and putrid prisons but its inventors, scientists, artists, writers and thinkers shaped how we live today.

Places To Go and Things To Do

Victorian London is still alive all around you! The Houses of Parliament and Lords Cricket Ground, the Albert Museum and Whitechapel Underground Station. The Victorians are everywhere.

An interesting project is to find out when your school or home was built. With a little bit of digging you can learn who lived in your home or founded your school. Your local library usually has a mine of info on the history of your area. Some of London's greatest buildings like the Houses of Parliament were built in Victorian times – why don't you see how many Victorian things you can spot on a walk round your high street?

THE SHERLOCK HOLMES MUSEUM at 221B Baker

Street, NW1 6XE. You can see the study where Holmes worked and the bedrooms of Holmes and Watson. Plus a selection of Sir Arthur Conan Doyle's letters. www.sherlock-holmes.co.uk. Tel 020 7935 8866.

Eat jellied eels, pie and mash just like a real Cockney costermonger at **M. MANZE**, 37 Tower Bridge Road, SE1 4TW. This is the oldest pie and mash shop in London – but be warned, its food, specially the squidgy bits, is definitely an acquired taste.

CARLYLE'S HOUSE, 24 Cheyne Road, Chelsea, SW3 5HL, was the home of the famous historian Thomas Carlyle, which was visited by friends such as Charles Dicken's and George Elliot. It has a beautiful Victorian walled garden. www.nationaltrust.org.uk. Tel 020 7352 7087.

Based on the house where Charles Dicken's wrote Oliver Twist, the DICKENS HOUSE MUSEUM, 48 Doughty Street, Bloomsbury WC1N 2LF, has a recreation of his bedroom as well as letters, sketches and objects that belonged to the great writer. It shows how he lived and worked. www.dickensmuseum.com. Tel: 020 7405 2127.

RAGGED SCHOOL MUSEUM, 46–50 Copperfield Road, Bow, E3 4RR, is based on what was London's biggest ragged school. It was open from 1877 to 1908 and thousands of London children were taught here. There are regular talks and event and your school can recreate real Victorian lessons (if you dare). www.raggedschoolmuseum.org.uk.

THE LONDON DUNGEON, 28–34 Tooley Street, London Bridge, SE1 2SZ, is a truly fascinating and gruesome museum. A font of grisly London history, its Victorian highlights include the horrible Jack the Ripper experience. www.thedungeons.com. Tel 020 7403 7221.

HIGHGATE CEMETERY, Swain's Lane, Highgate, N6 6PJ, was opened in 1839 – it's just down the road from Waterlow Park another Victorian creation. It has fantastic gravestones including those of Karl Marx, George Elliot and the Victorian scientist Michael Faraday.

ROYAL BOTANIC GARDENS, Kew, Richmond, TW9 3AB,

is the most famous botanic gardens in the world. It has some fantastic Victorian buildings including the amazing Palm House and the Water Lily House. www.rbg.kew.org.uk. Tel 020 8332 5655.

POLLOCK'S TOY MUSEUM, 1 Scala Street, W1 2HL,

offers a chance to see the kind of toy soldiers, teddy bears and wax figures that Victorian children played with. The toy theatres are the main attraction of this marvellous toy museum, which is named after the Victorian publisher Benjamin Pollock. www.pollocksweb.co.uk. Tel 020 7636 3452.

BETHNAL GREEN MUSEUM OF CHILDHOOD,

Cambridge Heath Road, E2 9PA, is lively and interesting museum that always seems to have something exciting on, from plays and puppet making to Christmas decorations. There's a great display of the history of toys – including some fantastic Victorian doll's houses. www.museumofchildhood.org.uk. Tel 020 8983 5200.

THE VICTORIA AND ALBERT MUSEUM, Cromwell

Road, South Kensington, SW7 2RL, is named after the monarch and her beloved husband. It is now one of the largest design museums in the world and has a stunning display of four centuries of costume and fashion. www.vam.ac.uk. Tel 020 7942 2000.

THE THEATRE MUSEUM, 1E Tavistock Street (entrance off Russell Street), Convent Garden, WC2E 7PA, is a great place to get to know the stars of the Victorian stage and music hall. This museum is packed with posters, costumes and reconstructions of early theatres. There are also displays on magic and the circus. www.theatremuseum.org. Tel 020 7943 4700.

MUSEUM OF LONDON, London Wall, EC2Y 5HN, is a wonderful place to learn all about London history. You can stroll down a Victorian street or stand in an eighteenth century prison cell. www.museumoflondon.org.uk. Tel 020 7600 3699.

BUCKINGHAM PALACE, St James's Park, SW1A 1AA, redesigned during Queen Vic's time, is still the official home of the royal family. You can visit the state rooms every August and September. www.royalresidences.com. Tel 020 7930 4832.

THE CUTTY SARK, King William Walk, Greenwich, SE10 9BG, was launched in 1869 and worked as a tea clipper – carrying tea across the high seas. In 1871 she completed the voyage from China to England in 107 days – which was a world record. You can now go aboard and see this perfectly preserved Victorian ship. www.cuttysark.org.uk. Tel 020 8858 3445.

Other books from Watling Street you'll love
In this series:

The Timetraveller's Guide to Roman London
by Olivia Goodrich
Find out just why Rome's craziest emperors invaded cool, cruel Britannia and built a city besides the Thames.
ISBN 1-904153-06-2

•

The Timetraveller's Guide to Saxon and Viking London
by Joshua Doder
Journey back to London when it was home to some of the funniest names and the foulest food in English history!
ISBN 1-904153-07-0

•

The Timetraveller's Guide to Medieval London
by Christine Kidney
Scratch, sniff and itch your way around the capital during its smelliest period in history.
ISBN1-904153-08-9

•

The Timetraveller's Guide to Shakespeare's London
by Joshua Doder
William Shakespeare is our greatest writer; read all about him, his plays and the big bad city he lived and worked in.
ISBN 1-904153-10-0

•

The Timetraveller's Guide to Tudor London
by Natasha Narayan
See the terrible tyrants, cruel queens, con men and cutpurses in Tudor London's dark, dingy and all too dangerous streets.
ISBN 1-904153-09-7

In case you have difficulty finding any Watling St books in your local bookshop, you can place orders directly through

BOOKPOST,
Freepost, PO Box 29, Douglas, Isle of Man IM99 1BQ

Telephone 01634 836000
email: bookshop@enterprise.net